CONNECTICUT

MASSACHUSETTS
RHODE ISLAND
NEW YORK
NEW YORK
Long Island Sound
HARTFORD
Enfield
Windsor
Vernon
Manchester
Mansfield
East Hartford
West Hartford
Newington
Glastonbury
New Britain
Bristol
Torrington
Putnam
Southington
Waterbury
Cheshire
Meriden
Middletown
Norwich
Naugatuck
Wallingford
New Milford
Danbury
Newtown
Hamden
New London
Groton
Shelton
New Haven
West Haven
East Haven
Branford
Trumbull
Milford
Stratford
Bridgeport
Fairfield
Westport
Norwalk
Stamford
Greenwich
Barkhamsted Reservoir
Nepaug Reserv.
Bantam L.
Bolton L.
Mansfield Hollow L.
Moodus Reserv.
Gardner L.
Pachaug Pond
Lake Candle-wood
Lake Gaillard
Saugatuck Reserv.
Housatonic R.
Farmington R.
Scantic R.
Willimantic R.
Shetucket R.
Quinebaug R.
Shepaug R.
Naugatuck R.
Connecticut R.
91
291
84
384
691
395
95
684
N
S
E
W
0
10 Miles
25 Miles
50 Miles
0
10 KM
25 KM
50 KM

CONNECTICUT

THE CONSTITUTION STATE

Michael Worek

FIREFLY BOOKS

A Firefly Book

Published by Firefly Books Ltd. 2025

First printing

Library of Congress Control Number: 2024947571

Library and Archives Canada Cataloguing in Publication
Title: Connecticut : the Constitution State / Michael Worek.
Names: Worek, Michael, author
Description: Includes index.
Identifiers: Canadiana 2024049086X | ISBN 9780228105459 (hardcover)
Subjects: LCSH: Connecticut—Guidebooks. | LCSH: Connecticut—Description and travel. | LCGFT: Guidebooks.
Classification: LCC F92.3 .W67 2025 | DDC 917.4604/44—dc23

Published in Canada by
Firefly Books Ltd.
50 Staples Avenue, Unit 1
Richmond Hill, Ontario
L4B 0A7

Published in the United States by
Firefly Books (U.S.) Inc.
P.O. Box 1338, Ellicott Station
Buffalo, New York
14205

Cover and interior design: Jacqueline Hope Raynor
Photo Editor: Cathy Hoshino

Printed in China | E

MIX
Paper | Supporting responsible forestry
FSC® C160794
FSC
www.fsc.org

INTRODUCTION

Although Connecticut is one of the smallest states in the Union, it is packed with history, culture and natural beauty. Rhode Island and Delaware cover a smaller geographical area, but Connecticut's more than 3,600,000 residents make it the fourth most densely populated state in the country. The state gets its name from the Connecticut River, and the word itself is derived from a Mohegan-Pequot word meaning "long tidal river."

European settlers began arriving in the area that would become Connecticut in the early 1600s. In 1639 they adopted a document called the Fundamental Orders as the basis of the colony's government. The Fundamental Orders are the first written constitution in the country and account for the state's official nickname, the Constitution State.

A group of Puritan settlers from the Massachusetts Bay Colony arrived in 1664 and the colony continued to grow. Connecticut was one of the thirteen colonies that declared independence from British rule and, after the American Revolution, Connecticut became the fifth state to ratify the constitution.

Today, Connecticut is home to many businesses and industries and to many excellent schools and universities, most notably Yale University in New Haven which was founded in 1701. Situated only 100 miles from New York City, the city is an ideal place to live with access to the amenities of New York while offering a smaller, more beautiful urban environment in which to live. Many residents commute to New York City daily.

The state's 600 miles of coastline provide ports and beaches and the state continues its maritime tradition. It is home to the Coast Guard Academy in New London.

With its rich history, natural beauty, ideal location and wide range of cities and towns, Connecticut truly offers something for everybody.

The Connecticut State Capitol Building, adjacent to Bushnell Park in Hartford, was designed by Richard Upjohn in the Eastlake style with elements of Victorian Gothic. Construction began in 1871 and the building opened in 1879. It was described at the time it opened as a vast mass of white marble that sparkles in the sunshine. The golden dome, illuminated at night, is still a city landmark.

This view of the skyline of downtown Hartford captures the city's business and commercial heart. Founded in 1635, Hartford is the capital of the state and one of the oldest cities in the United States. During the 19th century it was a center of industry and manufacturing and one of the wealthiest cities in the country. Today, it has a population of just over 120,000 and is home to Wadsworth Atheneum, the nation's oldest public art museum, and Bushnell Park, the nation's oldest publicly funded park.

PROUD TO BE AMERICAN

SACRED HEART UNIVERSITY'S
DISCOVERY
SCIENCE CENTER & PLANETARIUM

(Previous page) A beautiful autumn morning in Shelton along the Housatonic River captures the beauty of Connecticut's historic towns and countryside. English settlers established a settlement here in 1639 and present-day Shelton was incorporated as a city in 1915.

Sacred Heart University is one of the largest Catholic universities in New England. The Discovery Science Center in Bridgeport, one of the state's most popular hands-on science learning centers for children and adults, was affiliated with the university in 2021.

Located in Bristol, The New England Carousel Museum houses one of the largest permanent collections of historic carousel animals in the United States. Exhibits explain how the carousels worked and how the animals were carved.

(Right) Children can ride a working carousel that recalls the days of county fairs and traveling circuses.

St Cloud

The Beckley Blast Furnace in East Canaan was built in 1847 to produce pig iron and continued in operation until 1919. The massive stone structure, 40 feet tall and 30 feet long on each side at the base, is now the main attraction in the 12-acre Beckley Iron Furnace State Park.

(Right) The beautiful Blackberry River flows westward over the dam near the Beckley Iron Furnace.

The Hurd House in Woodbury with its massive central chimney, was originally two small houses. The original house was built for John Hurd, the town's miller, in 1680 and an extension was added in 1718. The house is now owned by the Old Woodbury Historical Society.

(Right) The famous Glass House in New Canaan was designed by Philip Johnson and completed in 1949. Situated on a very private lot, the house overlooks a pond and woods. Johnson lived in the house until his death in 2005. The house and its companion building, the Brick House, are now open to the public.

William Gillette (1853–1937) was an American stage actor who made his fortune playing Sherlock Holmes. Construction of the house began in 1914 and took five years. The house has three stories, 24 rooms and covers 14,000 square feet. The exterior is fieldstone, making it appear from a distance as if the house is crumbling away. The interior includes hand-crafted doors and trick locks, secret passageways and a grand staircase. Now a part of Gillette Castle State Park in East Haddam, the house was restored in 2002 and receives about 350,000 visitors a year. The covered footbridge (above) on the grounds of the castle leads to hiking trails and a picnic area.

Construction of Fort Griswold, now part of Fort Griswold Battlefield State Park in Groton, began in 1775 to control the entrance to the Thames River during the Revolutionary War. In 1781 British forces under the command of Benedict Arnold captured the fort in the Battle of Groton Heights.

(Right) Completed in 1830, the 135-foot-tall Groton Monument is dedicated to the soldiers who were killed in the Battle of Groton Heights.

OPEN

The Submarine Force Library and Museum is located on the Thames River in Groton. Among more than 30,000 items in the museum is the USS *Nautilus* (SSN-571) submarine, the first nuclear powered submarine in the world. It weighs 3,400 tons, is about the length of a football field and served from 1954 until 1985. The SSN-571 was designated Connecticut's State Ship in 1983. Other exhibits include midget submarines (right), working periscopes, a submarine control room and detailed models of submarines. More than 150,000 people visit the museum each year.

7
6
5
4
3
2
1
0

At The Dudley Farm Museum visitors can experience life in rural New England at the end of the 19th century. Also on the grounds is the Quinnipiac Dawnland Museum covering the history of the area's Indigenous population.

This historic covered bridge in West Cornwall crosses the Housatonic River and is 172 feet long and 15 feet wide. Built around 1864, entirely of wood, the bridge has been maintained and strengthened and continues today to handle limited traffic.

The Connecticut River divides the cities of Hartford and East Hartford and the bridges that cross it are an integral part of the cities transportation system. Since 1981, Riverfront Recapture, a nonprofit organization, has led public and private efforts to create parks and recreation areas on both sides of the river. The Connecticut is the longest river in New England and flows for over 400 miles from its source near the Canadian border in Vermont through four states until it reaches Old Saybrook on Long Island Sound. Despite its calm appearance as it flows through Hartford, the river discharges over 18,000 cubic feet of water into the Atlantic Ocean.

Alexander Calder's sculpture, *Stegosaurus*, is made from 45 thin steel plates bolted together in an abstract form representing a dinosaur from the Jurassic Period. The popular 50-foot-tall, red-orange sculpture was installed on the Alfred E. Burr Memorial Mall in 1973.

(Right) Made of stone and marble, the 30-foot-tall Corning Fountain was installed in 1899 at the entranceway to Bushnell Park. Indigenous people from the Saukiog tribe are representative of the area's original inhabitants.

WEST
84
NORTH
91

Founders Bridge in Hartford is a major artery into the city. The wide pedestrian walkway has become a favorite with residents and tourists and provides a perfect vantage point to admire the city skyline.

The Soldiers and Sailors Memorial Arch in Hartford commemorates the 4,000 citizens of the town who served in the Civil War. Dedicated in 1886, it is the first permanent memorial arch built in the United States.

(Left) Mark Twain (Samuel Langhorne Clemens) is one of America's most important authors. He lived in this house in Hartford from 1874 to 1891 and many of his most famous books, including *The Adventures of Tom Sawyer*, *Life on the Mississippi*, *Adventures of Huckleberry Finn*, and *A Connecticut Yankee in King Arthur's Court*, were written while he lived here. The building was declared a National Historic Landmark in 1962 and extensively restored in 2004.

The Connecticut Science Center in Hartford opened in 2009. The nine-story museum features interactive exhibits, videos, educational programs and live demonstrations intended to promote the study of science.

The New Britain Museum of American Art was the first museum dedicated solely to acquiring American art. The collection is known for its holdings in colonial portraiture, the Hudson River School, American Impressionism, the Ash Can School, and murals by Thomas Hart Benton.

This six-story International Style building houses the Beinecke Rare Book & Manuscript Library at Yale University in New Haven. Established with a gift from the Beinecke family, the library collection totals over one million books and several hundred thousand manuscripts. There are no exterior windows in the building, but the marble facade is only 1.25 inches thick and allows filtered sunlight to penetrate inside the building. The interior of the building (left) shows some of the six floors of books that are not in storage below ground. Among the many treasures preserved here are one of the 48 known copies of the Gutenberg Bible.

Ingalls Rink at Yale University in New Haven seats 3,500 spectators. A 295-foot reinforced concrete arch supports the roof. Commonly called the Whale because of its shape, the rink is home to the Yale Bulldogs hockey teams.

The Yale Bowl Stadium is home to the Yale Bulldogs college football team. This statue of the original bulldog sits outside the gates. The stadium opened in 1914 and can seat 61,000 fans.

Constructed in 1896 in the monumental Victorian Gothic style, Phelps Hall and Gate are the main entrance to the Yale University campus.

(Left) The New Haven townhouses that line Court Street were built in 1870. Located near Wooster Square and only 375 feet long, the single lane road is open to residents only. Trees, planters and benches give the area a small-town feel.

The Yale Center for British Art was established with a gift from Paul Mellon, Class of 1929. It houses the largest and most comprehensive collection of British art and artifacts in the United States. The building was designed by Louis Kahn and stands across the street from the Yale University Art Gallery.

(Left) Edward P. Evans Hall, the main building of the Yale School of Management, was opened in 2014. It is famous for its beautiful architectural design and the high quality of the art and finishes inside. The four-story building covers 230,000 square feet and includes an enclosed courtyard, classrooms, offices and meeting spaces.

This substantial Georgian red clapboard house with a massive central chimney set amidst ancient trees and stone walls captures the timeless appeal of much of New England.

(Right) When the land for Mount Tom State Park was donated to the state in 1911, a condition of the gift was that the state build an observation tower on the property. Mount Tom Tower, completed in 1921, stands 34 feet tall and is constructed from stone found on the site.

The beautiful Mashantucket Pequot Museum and Research Center is tribally owned. It contains exhibits, classrooms, an auditorium, conservation laboratories and multi-sensory dioramas. Tribal Nation are descended from the Pequot people. The Green Corn ceremony, being reenacted above, was held each year to ensure a good harvest of corn.

Connecticut's natural beauty has been enhanced by tasteful bridges, dams and ornamental architecture. The old stone bridge and waterfall at Case Mountain Recreational Area (left) and the Oriental Garden Pond (above) in Wickham Park are both found in Manchester.

Ripka's Beach Cafe is a favorite spot to eat and enjoy the view at Calf Pasture Beach.

(Right) The Captain William Clark Fishing Pier is the centerpiece of Calf Pasture Beach in Norwalk. The area was used by early settlers as grazing land for cows, giving the area its name. The British landed troops on the peninsula when they attacked and burned Norwalk in 1779 during the American Revolutionary War.

The First Congregational Church of Litchfield was founded in 1721. The current building, constructed in 1829, was modeled on St. Martin-in-the-Fields church in London, England. A major restoration was undertaken in 2005. The graves of early settlers (above) provide a record of Litchfield's earliest colonial inhabitants.

Mystic Seaport Museum, the largest maritime museum in the United States, receives about 250,000 visitors a year.

The heart of the museum is the collection of beautiful small wooden sailing, rowing and power boats, which are as elegant as they are functional.

Historic Mystic is one of the most visited places in Connecticut. In 1941 Mystic Seaport acquired the *Charles W. Morgan*, built one hundred years earlier in 1841, the last remaining wooden whaling ship in the world and built its extensive collection of ships and buildings from there. The tall masts of the *Morgan* dwarf the small lighthouse on Chubb's Wharf on the Mystic River.

Mystic features over 60 historic buildings, most moved to the site and carefully restored to capture the authentic flavor of what life was like in a seaport village in New England in the 19th century.

Mystic Aquarium houses the only beluga whales in captivity in New England in a 760,000-gallon pool. The aquarium's mission is to foster an interest in the conservation of the oceans of the world.

U S COAST GUARD

The ferry service between New London and Long Island, New York serves about one million passengers annually. At a speed of 15 knots, the *Mary Ellen* is one of the fastest ships in the fleet and makes the crossing in 40 minutes.

(Left) The United States Coast Guard Cutter *Eagle* is used to train Coast Guard officers and cadets in seamanship. Based in New London, the vessel is 295 feet long and carries 22,000 square feet of sail as well as a 1,200-horsepower diesel engine.

The twin spans of the Gold Star Memorial Bridge carry 11 lanes of traffic more than a mile across the Thames River between New London and Groton. It is the longest bridge and the largest structure in the state. The bridge was named in honor of the citizens of the area who were killed in World War I, World War II and the Korean War.

The Bruce Museum in Greenwich was established in 1912. The building was gifted to the town by Robert Moffat Bruce, a local industrialist. Today, the Bruce contains over 43,000 square feet of exhibition space showcasing its important holdings in paintings and sculpture, Indigenous history and culture, dioramas of Connecticut's natural landscape, birds and animals and extensive displays of local natural history.

the
Bruce

The headquarters of WWE (World Wrestling Entertainment), the world's largest professional wrestling promotion company, is located in Stamford.

The commute by train between Greenwich and New York City is only a little over an hour, allowing many residents to live in Connecticut but work in New York.

Noank is a picturesque village with a rich history at the mouth of the Mystic River in Groton. The historic district is listed on the National Register of Historic Places and includes houses and commercial buildings dating back to the 1840s.

(Right) The Morgan Point Lighthouse on the west side of the river, was built in 1868 and guided traffic in and out of the harbor until 1919 when it was decommissioned. It is now a private residence.

1868

Norwich, founded in 1659, is located on the Thames River. The city has been called the Rose of New England since the 1850s when the famous preacher Henry Ward Beecher visited the town and admired the many gardens there. Its historic city hall (right) evokes the city's pride in its long heritage.

CITY HALL

New England's long rural heritage is evident in the large red barns and stacked fieldstone walls seen throughout Connecticut. The area around Sanfordtown Road near Redding, where these buildings stand, is particularly rich in traditional rural architecture.

Salisbury was granted a town charter in 1741. The discovery of a large deposit of iron ore and the waterpower provided by the Great Falls Reservoir provided the industry that sustained the town's economic prosperity for over 200 years.

(Right) This historic grist mill stone sits at the site of the original iron-producing Salisbury Furnace.

Scoville Memorial Library in Salisbury was constructed with funds bequeathed to the town by Jonathan Scoville when he died in 1891. One of the oldest libraries in the United States, it was established in 1803 based on a collection of books formed in 1771.

(Left) Like so many of Connecticut's historic small towns, Salisbury is rich in period architecture that recalls the past but is lovingly maintained and used today

In the days of building with wood, bridges were covered with a roof so that the planks on the surface of the bridge did not rot. The Comstock Bridge in East Hampton, built in 1873, is one of the few original bridges to survive. It is now limited to pedestrian traffic.

(Left) Covered bridges are a popular attraction wherever they survive, but most have rotted away. A few, like this one at Stratton Brook State Park in Simsbury, is a modern recreation. It was built in 1985 using traditional design and materials.

Castle Craig in Hubbard Park provides an expansive view over Meriden. The tower is 32 feet high and was constructed in 1900 from locally sourced stone.

(Right) Camp Columbia State Park in Morris was formerly owned by Columbia University and used as a summer campus for engineering and surveying students. The Camp Columbia Tower was a gift from the Columbia University Class of 1906.

WINDHAM COVPT HOVSE
979 Main St
WINDHAM
TOWN HALL

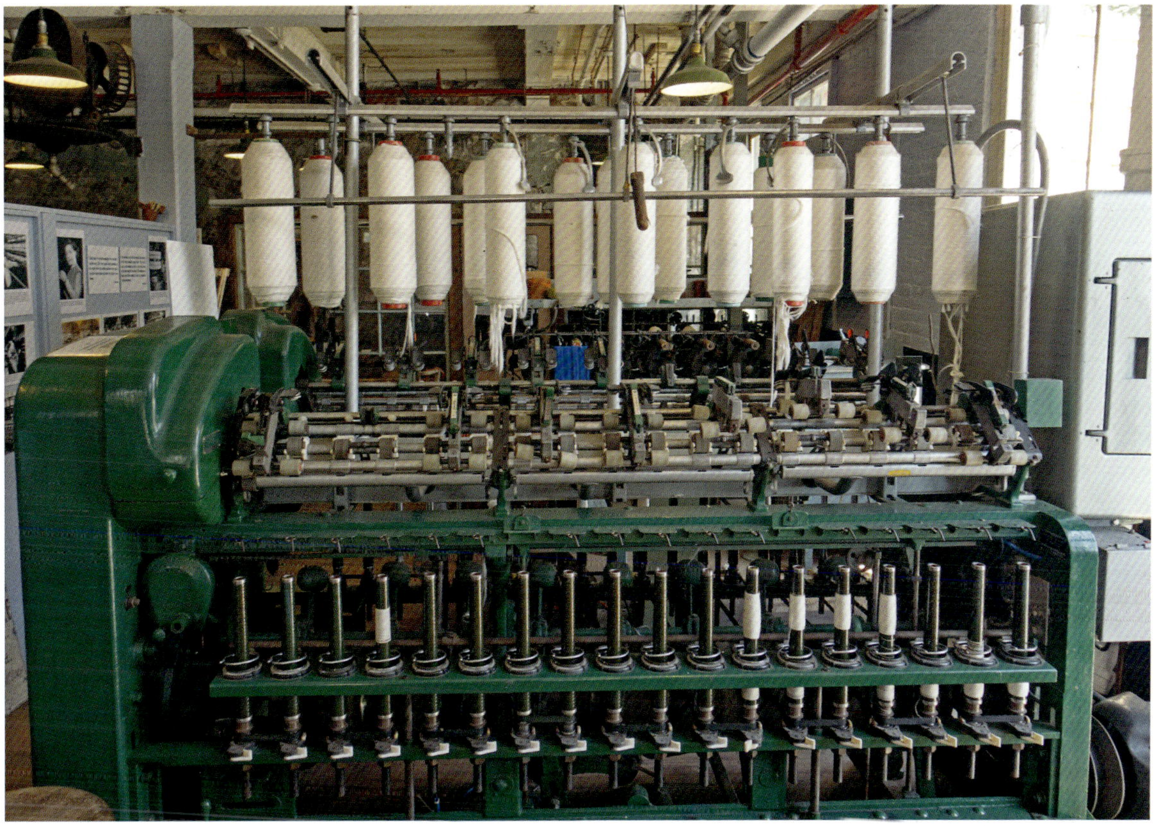

The Windham Textile and History Museum features the Brooke Shannon Antique Sewing Machine Room which includes machines from factories that would have been used at the end of the 19th century.

(Left) The history of the town of Windham dates to 1675. The construction of the beautiful town hall required more than one million red bricks when it was built in 1896. The availability of waterpower led to the establishment of early industries in Willimantic along the river.

The New England Air Museum in Windsor Locks features three display hangers that house aircrafts ranging from early flying machines to supersonic jets. Aircraft on display include this fighter bomber from the Second World War.

This Lockheed 10A Electra from the 1930s is similar to the aircraft used by aviation pioneer Amelia Earhart.

The stained-glass windows at the Cathedral of St. Joseph in Hartford are approximately 70 feet high and 14 feet wide. The cathedral, built in 1962, can seat 1,750 people. The result is a Gothic cathedral made with modern materials.

In contrast to the Cathedral of St. Joseph, Greenfield Hill Congregational Church in Fairfield was constructed in 1855 in the classic New England style. The traditional elements of white and clean lines blend to create an interior of great beauty and simplicity.

Harkness Memorial State Park in Waterford was established in 1950. The estate was left to the state by Mary Harkness whose father-in-law, an early investor in Standard Oil, built the 42-room mansion, which he called Eolia, as a summer home in 1906. The park contains over 220 acres and offers mansion tours, picnicking, hiking and shoreline fishing. The property is listed in the National Register of Historic Places.

Despite its wealth of historic buildings, small towns and vibrant cities, it is the beauty of the countryside that attracts many visitors to the state. Walking trails abound and the countryside is inviting all year round.

PHOTO CREDITS

ALAMY

Rainer Lesniewski: 2; Randy Duchaine: 14; Randy Duchaine: 15; Stan Tess: 16; Mark Hertzberg/ZUMA Press Wire: 19; Tom Croke: 24; Stan Tess: 25; Kenneth Grant: 31; Stan Tess: 36; Stan Tess: 37; Michael Rooney: 44; Randy Duchaine: 48; George Ostertag: 51; George Oze: 60; Clarence Holmes Photography: 62; Clarence Holmes Photography: 63; Jon Arnold Images Ltd: 64–65; Patti McConville: 69; Richard Cummins: 70; Randy Duchaine: 72; Stan Tess: 73; Albert Knapp: 74; Albert Knapp: 75; Miro Vrlik Photography: 76; Yakoniva: 77; Kumar Sriskandan: 78; Alpha Stock: 79; George Ostertag: 83; Stan Tess: 84; Randy Duchaine: 85; Danita Delimont: 86; Danita Delimont: 87; Stan Tess: 90; Stan Tess: 91; Randy Duchaine: 96

SHUTTERSTOCK

Sean Pavone: 6–7; Sean Pavone: 8–9; LBSimms Photography: 10–11; Ritu Manoj Jethani: 12; Ritu Manoj Jethani: 13; Shanshan0312: 17; LEE SNIDER PHOTO IMAGES: 18; Harry Collins Photography: 20; Alexey Stiop: 21; Actium: 22; Rachel Rose Boucher: 23; Rachel Rose Boucher: 26; Jennifer Yakey-Ault: 27; Jay Yuan: 28–29; James Kirkikis: 30; Sean Pavone: 32; f11photo: 33; Brian Logan Photography: 34; f11photo: 35; Jose L Vilchez: 38; Winston Tan: 39; Ritu Manoj Jethani: 40; Chad Robertson Media: 41; Jon Bilous: 42; Little Vignettes Photo: 43; Ritu Manoj Jethani: 45; Richard Cavalleri: 46; Shanshan0312: 47; Miro Vrlik Photography: 49; Elizabeth C Waters: 50; Miro Vrlik Photography: 52; Laura Stubbs: 53; Shanshan0312: 54; Dan Hanscom: 55; Actium: 56; singh_lens: 57; Ritu Manoj Jethani: 58; James Kirkikis: 59; Actium: 61; 365 Focus Photography: 66–67; JHVEPhoto: 68; TheBrassGlass: 71; CJY Images: 80; Jeremy J Coute: 81; Little Vignettes Photo: 82; James Kirkikis: 88; James Kirkikis: 89; Steven Kornfeld: 92; ARENA Creative: 93

INDEX

The *Boys of Summer* penguin sculpture sits in front of the New Britain Museum of American Art.